Loving the Dead

Poems by
Helga Kidder

BLUE LIGHT PRESS ◆ 1ST WORLD PUBLISHING

1ST WORLD
PUBLISHING

SAN FRANCISCO ◆ FAIRFIELD ◆ DELHI

Winner of the 2020 Blue Light Press Book Award

Loving the Dead

BLUE LIGHT PRESS
www.bluelightpress.com
bluelightpress@aol.com

1ST WORLD PUBLISHING
PO Box 2211
Fairfield, IA 52556
www.1stworldpublishing.com

BOOK & COVER PHOTO & DESIGN
Melanie Gendron
melaniegendron999@gmail.com

COVER ART
"The Critic" by Melanie Gendron

AUTHOR PHOTO
KB Ballentine

FIRST EDITION

Library of Congress Control Number: 2020936688

ISBN: 9781421836577

In memory of my sister,
Gerlinde B. Wenzel, 1941-2018

Contents

Searching for Answers

Visiting the Dream House 1

One Day Closer 2

Searching for Answers 3

Rivers of Living Water 4

Walking to Town for Tapas 5

Under the Blood Moon 6

Valentine 7

Beware of What You Wish For 8

Hungry Mother State Park 9

Ash Wednesday 10

Leaning Toward the Light 11

Snow Moon 12

Purging 13

Seventy-Fifth Birthday 14

Mending 15

Schadenfreude 16

Launching a New Year 17

Bearing the Light 18

Moon Mystery 19

When You Doubt Heaven 20

Praise 21

Rain Recites the Laws of Loss

Loving the Dead 25

When Breath Becomes Air 26

Memory's Closet 27

May the ground be like feathers to you 28

Scattering Seeds 29

One Cold February Night 30

Talking to the Dead 31

White Lavender, ... 32

At Lake Constance 33

Sunflower Next to Your Grave 34

Your Picture in My Hand 35

Barometer of Absence 36

Villanelle for the Dead 37

The Departed 38

Dance of the Dead 39

Appleing in Your Nikes 40

Forgiveness is Like Light 41

Miracle Moments 42

Night Watch 43

Flood 44

The Dance of Forgotten Souls

Blue 47

La Lumiere 48

Je Suis Parisienne 49

At St. Mary's Convent, Sewanee, TN 50

My Brother's Ghost 51

Flash Flood 52

Waiting all Summer 54

Luna Moth 55

Dance of the Forgotten 56

Driving through Chickamauga Battlefield 57

Thanksgiving 58

Day in Fall 59

Weaving the Future 60

Love is a Power Word 61

Faith 62

Wildfire on Walden's Ridge 63

Breathing 64

Shadows, Darkening 65

September 9, 2001 66

Stars Shine on Everyone 67

Last Song 68

Acknowledgements 69

About the Author 71

Searching for Answers

in winter's darkest corner.
Light waits at the door.

Visiting the Dreamhouse

Under a bruised moon rain plays
sonatas at my window of sleep.
I walk a trail of comets
arcing toward earth.

Closer, in woods, gnats cloud the moon's path.
Beneath my feet dead leaves curl.
Wind brews a storm
inside me
                where a horse whinnies.
Reigns in your right hand, the left
you extend to me.

But I heard the train's rhythm on tracks,
smell engine steam,
that metal whiff of steel.
And I climb the steps
to the past.

One Day Closer

Morning fog crawls over the ridge,
a toddler learning to walk.
Closer, air whirls birds
where feeders hang like lanterns
that prod morning light.

Mid-day, the lounge chair poolside
longs to fit my curve, so I sit
and stick my fork into the plate's offering,
watch a red-bibbed grosbeak
stop for a snack.

At evening, the sky purples
like a giraffe's tongue, quivers,
and flicks stars into space
sweet as the treats parents promise
children at bed-time.

Time Stayeth Not,
the grandfather clock face said
to my ancestors as they sailed
along the coast
to find their home.
Tonight, the clock strikes for me.

Searching for Answers

As your words lean into me,
morning winds lisp in sourwood.
My answer stumbles over stone. It is not easy
to love the planet our lives have become.
Mourning doves carry my dreams
in pines, caught in branches.
Light thick on the horizon.
Do clouds know where they are thrust?
As time grinds river rock into sand,
stars sip the darkness,
and dreams are held in a self-made prison.
Undertow gathers light's desire,
crumples against the solid shore.
Spume lifts hands in prayer.

Spume lifts hands in prayer,
crumples against the solid shore.
Undertow gathers light's desire
and dreams are held in a self-made prison.
Stars sip the darkness
as time grinds river rock into sand.
Do clouds know where they are thrust?
Light thick on the horizon,
in pines, caught in branches.
Mourning doves carry my dreams
to love the planet our lives have become.
My answer stumbles over stone. It is not easy
as morning winds lisp in sourwood
and your words lean into me.

Rivers of Living Water
John 7:38

Words harbor split personalities.
Some falter in the light of discovery.

Sometimes words whip and lash your back
or they tell you that sugar maple
surges sap to roots
if your hands touch bark
or your breath envelops branches.

There is a river flowing inside you
carrying words like shards
or time-worn pebbles.

Sometimes the river
floats words like paper lanterns,
but the right words seldom arrive
on time.

Walking to Town for Tapas

in Granada, Spain
after Federico Garcia Lorca

Like love
cobblestones re-educate
my body

lead me
to the Plaza del Carmen,
where fountains shower
arid night air

and the moon's cold fingers
stroke
sycamore leaves,

but women in the Plaza stand
hands on hips,
provoking night.

Under the Blood Moon

He is asleep in the bedroom upstairs.
She watches television, a woman
trying to convince the jury
of her innocence. An owl complains
in pines behind the house. Down
the road neighbors rest in double beds.
Their dog howls at a siren passing.

For thirty-five years she has learned
to live in the Tennessee hills
with wood creatures and vermin.
She remembers screaming as child
at a spider scaling the wall.

She thinks now of German railways
gliding through the Black Forest,
the ticket she will have to buy
visiting family and her sister's
fresh grave.

She also remembers love
as she had imagined it.
Not like this moon, shining
on whomever he wants.

Valentine

Spring traps winter like a mouse.
Jessamine on the verge of a gold-scented blast
scales the arbor.
Where fallen leaves smothered phlox,
soft rains douse loam awake.

You coax my shoulder closer
loosening yesterday's grip,
thunder clouds feathering out.
Lento, lento murmurs blood
tonguing a bridge between us.
Sheets sweet-hay harvest.

Spring paints shades of light,
a concert of violin and flute.
Earth trilling.

Beware of What You Wish For

At three a.m. the moon traps my face,
blinds eyes, drags me
through window and bare branches
as I inhale the clear night sky.

Shivering alone amid celestial crags
and ridges, ground wind blows
through me like a winter tree.

I see earth's blue and white ball
where hearts play games,
where I live deep inside myself
tethered to lunar reins.

As child I longed for the moon,
not aware of its dependence.

Hungry Mother State Park

Virginia

Green is yellower here.
The hills, too, curve more gently.
Great gray clouds finally rain.
Once inside the cabin, no TV.
Re-acquaint yourself
with a strange bed,
its breath,
the suck, suck
that like a hunger
attaches to the spine
the second you relax.
Your pulse steadily slows
from the week's race.
Hungry Mother.
A woman starving
for more than words.
On yesterday's TV you watched
a mountain climber fall
into a crevasse.
He could not climb up.
He could only lower himself
to the darkness,
to the unknown,
a station between gravity
and flight, hope,
what he wished for
at the bottom:
A passage to the light.
You want that faith.

Ash Wednesday

Vestments purple, the priest
signs my forehead
with a cross of ashes,

body already a microbial zoo,
harboring trillions of bacteria.

Ashes from heaven knows what
seeping deep into skin,
perhaps into my brain

as it translates poems
to knitting needles purling
a winter sweater.

Each row loops words
given up, each pattern
a haiku lost.

Poetry passions my body,
hooks my hands
like an ardent rogue.

Fearful of touch,
I am the distant moon,
skirt of passion faded like youth
when plums juiced my mouth
and *beauty is truth,*
truth beauty.

———————

*lines from *Ode on a Grecian Urn* by John Keats

Leaning Toward the Light

Summer caught a butterfly in my hands:
Large, golden, black-winged,
still testing the wind.

Fall returned me home
for a class reunion. Promises
fluttered from table to table.

Winter carries the sentence
imposed by summer and fall:
A notch of gold, a bundle of words.

Snow Moon

Kneeling on top of the ridge, the sun prays
over the moon and stars,
then blinds them to rest.

How long will the sun and the moon endure?
How long the heart that zig-zags
through wild grass, slides over ice,
pierces the flesh of love?

This morning I chased a calico away
from feeding birds,
shadowed our dog to the mailbox,
picked the news off the driveway,
poured you a cup of coffee.
You buttered the toast.

We know rain licks dust after drought,
snow muffles a noisy world,
the moon's frozen face chills the body.

The heart, though deceitful,
will decode its roots.

Purging

Flush out the sins,
insatiable appetite, the hurt
the world offers.

Yet all that lives
fights to be first in line,
for the best angle of sun.

This morning I witnessed a cardinal
clawing a wren at the feeder.
I drank a cup of coffee, extra-strong,
to quicken my step,
to stay ahead of the hours.

But without time
pain, sorrow, tough luck
would stay on hold forever.

Expel the indiscretions,
words spoken behind the back,
times we shrugged off
the still small voice inside us,
shaking its forefinger
in our proud faces.

Seventy-fifth Birthday

for Susanne

Good wishes, written in sand for me
at the beach of Fuerteventura
where you straddle waves.

You sent me Mario de Andrade's poem
all the way from Spain to Savannah
where Spanish moss hangs like a veil
over the beloved.

Here the cat meows at the door
and the puppy paws my knee
while morning sun lounges in the lawn,
plays hide and seek in living oaks.

I'd like to think I'm still in summer,
yet fall reveals a tree's true self,
the bare bones of being.

De Andrade writes, *life is a plate of candies.*
Have I eaten mine too fast?
I listen to the whispers inside me
browsing the last handful
before the veil frays
into a shroud.

Mending

Wish I could pull thread through ore,
sew close the rift between us:
The rip in my cotton shift I finger.

I douse our thirsty garden
as morning bees hum and stitch clusters
of blue salvia and silver lace vine
hugging the wrought-iron railing.

Bees begin needling blooms at dawn
after the sun's fingers stroke
each flower awake, warm nectar
for their daily thimble full.

Golden and purple finch brush
bronze maiden grass, baste air
as I spy a morning glory volunteer:
Blue trumpets loop the feeder pole.

I call to you inside,
begin patching the frayed gap.

Schadenfreude

When pride steps over caution,
history repeats itself.

Nightly we walk the hundred steps
of consciousness to the flood of stars.

We carry the fury of light
in and out of waking, the way
birds rend the days
in circles, ellipses, rectangles.

We crouch behind our walls,
refuse to shatter boundaries
while the world gloats.

Each night the moon
slows our race against time
as we try to live inside it.

Then we remember words
the decade demanded
and how their weight lifted us.

Launching a New Year

Midnight fireworks pop and flare
a new year. The moon, round and still
in its lit cloak, surveys the first hours
you dream away.

Sourwood and sweetgum fissure
the sky's dawning horizon.
Early birds flitter toward feeders
barely seeded after last night's raid.

A new year growing strong and bold
like winter sun imprinting branches,
twining through laurel and yew.

You stir and pull covers closer.
Last year's tarnished soul
forgotten.

Bearing the Light

Day stretches the color of pale honey
and she is happy, tasting the roses
in full bloom, tomatoes finally ripe,
grape vines twining the fence.

This thing within, like bees humming
through her body, her veins, her heart —
no one and nothing can take away.

Not his frowned brow,
not the hammer in her knee
knocking each time her foot bears down.
Not the river running through her
carrying debris and wreckage.

Moon Mystery

A coyote's howl runs down the spine
of the October moon.

His full face strikes my path —
a frigid forest that sips rain,
then weeps.

Once I watched a tropical bird court his love
moonwalking a branch:
A smooth glide backward, forward.

Blue or full, sickle or cradle,
waxing, waning, the moon surges my room
with his cool, pale light,
then slowly moves on.

When You Doubt Heaven

Impossible to regain passion now
that winter has stripped trees bare,
frost whitened meadows,
and winds shiver through forests.
Raccoons raid bird feeders
and owls hoot midnight closer.

No time to dwell on absence.
Poetry sifts my complaint.
Daily routines comfort hands
holding spoon, needle, or pen,
let love rise to the surface,
spread like jam on daily bread.

Praise

After snow and freeze, a lone jonquil flares
a bright light at the wood's edge.
The moon's fullness fading, a witness.

You've finally grown into yourself,
mapped out your own paradise,
the yoke you chose early,
nightly dreams stiffening your backbone,
lining your tongue with soft words.

You must be a minor god
creating with your hands and body
little miracles
that drizzled your years with sweetness.

Gusts push a bank of clouds over the ridge,
darkening the day.
You must turn on your own light.

In Spring's revival
Rain Recites the Laws of Loss.
Tomorrow hope reigns.

Loving the Dead

The cardinal said, *she lives*
between the sun and the moon,
within the light of stars.

Each rose petal says,
she is here, opening the flower
to perfection. Her voice
whispering the wind,
unfolding your heart.

The mirror reflects her shadow
behind you. *Don't grieve.*
You are not alone.

Not in the woods or fields.
Not in the city.
She is turning down her bed
inside you.

When Breath Becomes Air

Meadowsweet mist rises like incense
at the afternoon's altar
as if angels played a thousand harps,
reminding of the scale of your laughter
on your last birthday. I called you
between cake and champagne.

Now your soul lives in lightning
flashing trees and houses,
in dreams, floating breathless
through air, and in the moon, blue.
Dancing.

Memory's Closet

Here they hang, memories
like notes of the blues,
that return time
as if it were yesterday.

Mother's teal knit two-piece
I saved from the Good Will pile.

My sister's lapis velvet cape
she left behind at her last visit.

I crave memory's touch,
the scent of fabric in my hands,
the shape of who they were.

Memory feeds and sustains
their songs inside me.

As if I sit in bare branches,
like the blue bird this morning,
waiting for a turn at the feeder.

May the ground be like feathers to you.
  — Russian Proverb

Your spirit still lives in my phone
or hides in the ocean between continents.
I read your saved messages,
re-live the conversations between us.

As the clock stalked time,
you slipped to eternal life
while a murder of crows clapped wings,
the wind prowled around the house,
and the last words that lined your lips
hung like frost tracing stubble:
Just let me sleep
so I can heal.

Memory stumbles over the past,
cannot re-shape it, only build
on doubts for the future.

Scattering Seeds

The chain of family suddenly broken,
we walk to your new home.

Pointing at the hamlet of graves
the child asks, *Who lives here?*

We tell her, those who live
behind the clouds
and spin rain into seeds
scattered into memory.

The child looks up,
I can't see anyone.

We stop in front of the stone,
your carved name below mother's
who waited for thirty years.

Underneath, an empty space
like the hollow inside us
we pray rain will fill.

One Cold February Night

The moon, purple-bruised,
jumps over shrubs like hurdles,
over furrows of flickering ashes,
the fire I rode for weeks.

Flames sing hymns of survival,
tease me into the warm circle,
wrap around my shoulders.

Drawn to the fire,
the golden flame, I allowed
red tendrils to burn within.

Flame stitches singe my heart.

Talking to the Dead

Last winter snow whipped yews
into serpents raising their white fangs,
dripping milky venom
as the world carves our flesh,
whittles down bones.

We walk the roads of sleep
trying to fight disasters,
meet the dead
mouthing solutions in a language
we hear but can't understand.
They raise arms
we can reach but not hold.

Now summer crouches
behind the garden door.
I hang fuchsia, their purple bells
inside drooping red blooms
shaped for the narrow beaks
of hummingbirds.

I am waiting for their wings
humming a love song
I will know.

White Lavender,

the song you and I harmonized
on Sundays after supper
while drying the dishes
mother washed.

You soprano, I alto,
we erased the week's niggling
and bickering between us,
brought mother's face to a smile.

Memory leaps over years
like a new lamb rousted
from napping in hay.

White lavender infuses
spring air, embraces
the sweet scent of memory.

At Lake Constance

The majesty of swans glides
over the lake's silk.

Underneath a weeping willow
we swing in the sun,
sip juice with soda,
glasses slippery in our hands,
remember the last time
you walked with us
along the lake's shore.

Is your foot print
still a remnant
on today's path?

Church bells chime the hour,
reminder time ticks relentlessly.

Fog haloes distant Alps.
Closer, gulls bicker.
Boats, planed for winter,
lie silent.

Sunflower Next to Your Grave

Seed caught in a rift of stones,
off-spring of a star's corona,
I stand as tall as you,
face turning with the sun's hours
in the day's scuff, shuffle, and leap.

You don't know the jaundiced sheen
of my soul, the tattoos storms needled
on frayed whorls and heart leaves.

Your face gold-leafs the loss
I weave through weeping willows.

Your Picture in My Hand

. . . constellations whispering like runes
in a cryptic language . . .
— Diane Frank

Not the sun peeling the day's layers,
not runes bursting constellations
writing the tongue.

Way down in a dying star's memory
of brightening the universe
you still stand behind the garden fence,
gripping flesh-colored slats
to steady your smile.

Not the tip of a cigarette burning lungs,
not the furry swish
of a squirrel's scratch and dig.

The moment love's rose grew
petals inside me,
nectar infused vessels and veins.

Not the wind-willed flame of a candle,
only a shadowed field at dusk,
hushed like your face
when the heart held its breath,
forgot drumming your chest.

Barometer of Absence

after Marilyn Kallet

I will carry you in my willow basket
to the market's offerings,
to the post office package counter,
to the knit shop, begin
knitting your sparkle into my new wrap,
the Chrysanthemum design.
I will blend and pour you into the iron skillet's
Dutch Pancake breakfast,
carry you to the altar of today's sermon,
sampling my handful of past,
spinning tears in my mouth.

There is a limit to carrying absence,
the lead heaviness
pushing me down
the sinkhole of loss,
but I will chase you
in the hummingbird's wingbeat,
in the hum of the bee
needling blooms.

Thirty years ago,
on mother's passing,
your words comforted me
like the rainbow's promise.
But now . . .

Villanelle for the Dead

Tonight wind whimpers as witness
disguising between batten and board
the departed pleading for forgiveness.

When you cross the river's thickness,
you left me behind at the gush of oars.
Tonight wind whimpers as witness.

Are you returning from death's finesse,
a possibility we often underscored,
if the departed plead for forgiveness?

Whom do the wall's voices possess
or the waves of moondust roar
while wind whimpers tonight as witness?

Last night I dug earth in darkness,
filled holes with rose roots that hoard
the departed pleading for forgiveness.

If you are here, brush or turn my pages
or flicker the candle's flame with hope.
Tonight the wind whimpers as witness,
but the departed don't plead for forgiveness.

The Departed

In a world of vapors
time flaps in the wind
like linens on a clothesline,
where the dark vessels of our minds
taste the light of stars,
where souls sail the universe of silence.

At times they stand beside us
in the kitchen as we peel potatoes
or cut onions for a salad,
wiping an errant tear.

They hover over us
when turning down the bed,
share our pillow,
embrace us in dreams.

As wind gropes at the future,
I see the moon's door open.
Stars blink codes
of love for the departed,
coils around my heart
like the tendrils of jessamine
after spring rain opens golden flutes.

Dance of the Dead

(Savannah, Georgia)

Last night the walls spoke to me
in taps and scratches as the wind blew
and branched bushes against the house.

Here, history hoards spirits that whisper
two-hundred-year-old stories of wars,
soldiers and slaves. Here, nights host
the dance of the dead.

You lightly stroked my hand
until I woke, puzzled
over meaning.

Did you finally lose fear of height,
soaring over the Atlantic through air?
Did you want to comfort me?
Or did your touch say,
Here I am. Come.

Appleing in Your Nikes

My feet slip easily into the beds,
golden wings on both sides.

Ambling through the orchard,
wind blows around my shoulders,
shoes slightly loose on my feet
weaving a waiting song
for your return.

I always wanted to walk in your shoes,
teachers holding you up
in my flushed face as good example.

Inhale the trees' apple yellow
and read – Winesap, Golden Delicious.
Taste the crisp fall day.

Driving home on Summer City Road,
rolling hills wind through fog
to the light-possessed day below.

Like Nike, I fly oceans
carrying the message of victory
over grief.

Forgiveness is Like Light

when fog lifts off the ridge
and drizzle awakens bulbs and branches
and the lake spools the sun
in gold and silver threads . . .

when the dim flicker
in your brain's bower connects
to the current of thought,
sheds luster on the color of angel wings
when a sudden intent of goodness
pardons your soul . . .

when after rain, an arc of color
appears in the sky so that God's promise
imprints and lightens your heart,
the way pear trees in March
brighten the winter-barren field . . .

when at the finish of your journey
a glow guides your final steps
through the tunnel of life,
when you enter the light,
become pierced
with the radiance of stars . . .

Miracle Moments

As shadows glide through the garden,
tea roses hold buds tight,
and squirrels rush through fallen leaves,
carrying seeds to their nests.

Oleander, nandina, hibiscus huddle
inside for winter until spring sun
wakens them again to flower.

One cricket found its way
to the corner behind the door,
chirps good luck through the house.

Birds wing time from trees to feeder.
Wind whispers the past
in juniper branches, bending.

All summer I watched the river flow,
how one rock divided it into two
like decisions made at crossroads.

Like the cloth of hope I wear,
densely woven into the future.

Night Watch

When the dark forest calls us
for departure, we chafe
against silver-barked birches,
needle-spiked firs, unbind
the straight jacket of life.

Skin tinges green
as the forest transforms us,
tacks our wills on trunks,
branches our desires
into leaf mold.

No light beam guides us
beyond our bodies. No eyes
lash the fire of coals.
We simply release our tongues' arrows
as earth unfolds her words.

Flood

Rain pours its story over the city
while I browse through time.
I try on memories I hoped to slim into,
slip into hours that spread and lengthen.
I believe mirrors lie and time thins
the moments I spent with you.
Moments tatted like lace,
tiny holes in between.
Time folds itself over, keeps memory
nestled inside cinch and re-fit
when rain recites the laws of loss,
swells the heart.

November fog veils
the Dance of Forgotten Souls.
Memory timeless.

Blue

after Robert Morgan

July is the blue month. In Tennessee
bluebirds throat matins as day struts time
through the hills. Leaves begin mourning,
having lost spring months ago. Bluegrass
strains circle front porch rockers where
sweet tea ices tongues and hydrangeas
loosen their grips in tinted hues of smoke.
Tropical rains cool tree tents for an hour,
prompt hosta fronds to raise faint heads.
Along roads wild wisteria twines like grapes,
climbs higher than children needing to touch
the sky. Day deepens to an ocean above
floating cloud islands until night's lapis darkens
rooms, unlatches doors for tomorrow's souls.

La Lumiere

— *Les Canadiens* by Cheryl Fortier

Light dances the river,
skips between coin-shaped leaves
that fleck the river golden.

Two boats float parallel but off-set,
one content in shadow,
the other lifted by light.

This is Auvillar, city of light
that bounces off white-washed houses,
flickering the Garonne at mid-day.

Brush strokes reach deep
underneath the surface,
carry small shafts of light to the bottom

where the river bleeds into earth
remembering the light,
lives swallowed out of season.

Je Suis Parisienne

Last stop before *Place Pigalle*, the Metro surfaces
from the city's underworld.

Morning is hopeful. Sun warms pedestrians,
airs comforters and pillows.

A tour guides me to *Sacre Coeur*.
Pray? For Whom? You, who machine-gunned
a theater-full of patrons, splattering their lives
like refuse over seats and floor?

To stand helpless. To have to close the door
behind what seemed perfectly good lives.

As if standing at a summit's edge
before letting go for the free fall.

After climbing a thousand steps,
sun lifts fog like a petition off the Seine.

The city mourns ashes,
triumphs in light.

At St. Mary's Convent, Sewanee, TN

Wouldn't it be easy to die here
my friend says, looking
on forests of aspen and oak
fall brushes with golden haloes.
Charcoal clouds striate the sky
as wind pinches leaves to let go.

Wonder who named the roads
we've left behind,
Rattlesnake Springs Lane,
Rule of St. Benedict Circle,
Angels' Rest.

Here we learn how to grow
edible landscaping: Plant Jerusalem
artichoke next to marigold,
nasturtium between squash,
allium among Red Russian kale.

Ora et labora – the nuns believe
in prayer and work. Hands seeding dirt,
seeds lifted to heaven
as leafy plants, flowers, all edible
kinds of prayer.

A nun, bent over the bar
of a walker strolls her tabby,
perched on the seat like a lady in waiting,
through the hall leading to the door,
showing us the way.

My Brother's Ghost

for Dieter

He plods among Black Forest firs
like a bear wakened from winter sleep,
boots heavy on moss and leaf carpet.
He strokes each trunk as if testing it
for felling ripeness, doesn't see
a stick bug sucking sap or a butterfly
lighting on a seedling. Like a young man
he strides and holds his axe ready,
scent of wood dust circling his blood.
And as if lost and searching for answers
in a slip of blue where birds chirr praise,
that night he finds the moon, sliced
in halves, one light, one dark,
and sinks into the hollow cry of loss.

Flash Flood

after Marie Howe

It doesn't matter that the sugar maple is leaning
closer to the house, that the cluster of seeds
I planted yesterday will wash away.

Something doesn't add up.
The dishwasher still leaks after repair,
wrens nest in the window box, and the cardinal
rules the bird feeder. Another woman
gives her unborn to the knife.

February is too wet. Each day spiders crochet
webs like bridges across the living room windows
I have to unravel. The mailbox shuts its mouth
to good news. The neighbor's cat prowls in yews.
The flag wraps itself around the pole.
Another soldier is ambushed and gunned down.

The house creaks and settles ghosts.
Weeds shoot up like fences.
Rain lakes in the wheelbarrow, rusts.
We close the garden door, but at night we hear
brisk wind shaking its lock. Another parent forgot
the baby in the car.

Ants squeeze through cracks, trail the kitchen floor.
I watch you cut crepe myrtle to stumps,
then leaving tiny heaps of dirt on the tile inside.
The toaster oven grows crumb-like calluses.
The lamp's socket hangs loose.
Wet cold lies over the woods.
Another shooter kills six people.

There is nothing we can do.
It is a year no different from any other.
We sit in front of the fire rubbing hands together
as rain floods and drowns wishes,
children and pets.
Nothing can bring any of them back.

Waiting all Summer

Wavelets of water glide through my hands
and feet as if I unrolled a bolt of silk.

A harem of birds flits to and from feeders
cattycorner to fuchsias I hung for you.

Listen to the knock, knock of hammers
raising the walls of a new house next door.

The Japanese maple spins leaves to gold.

How often we walk in our own fires,
forget about the burn afterwards.

An owl sharpens his claws in soft rain.

Fuchsias opened purple flutes
shaped for your needle beak.

If I hold a mirror to your green throat,
I read your plea for survival.

My heart's warm springs flood
like the rare Fiji flower
that cries in her sleep.

Luna Moth

You must have escaped the moon's craters,
pale green wings ethereal
as a fairy's, landing on the rose bush,
reminding me of moments lost
treading the world's wheel.

What brings you to my garden?
Your four painted eyes on wings look at me
as if seeking refuge. I sigh,
want to open my vault of mercy
to your endangered species.

You will perfume the air
for mating, then leave behind eggs
for a new generation
as the first leaves of fall,
brown and brittle from drought,
dwindle to the ground.

Dance of the Forgotten

Winter wind whines through woods,
whips and tosses flakes around tree trunks
like refugees begging for shelter.

Where can they go except fall
into the ground or sink
and drown in a foreign sea?

Tonight they cling to naked branches,
pine needles, and magnolia leaves
willing to lend a rill or crag, thankful.

But the wind scrapes roofs and shrubs,
whirls all in air for a final, *tough luck – no room,*
dizzying, mind-altering waltz.

Driving through Chickamauga Battlefield

— in memory of George Russell Kidder
(1842 – 1866)

History rises through deciduous brush
and scrub pines to a waxing moon
as I roll past soldiers buried
nearly two centuries ago.

Your mind sharp as a whittle knife
when a bullet pierced your skull.
You returned home, fathered one child,
then hung your life on a rope.

Monuments and markers kneel at the edge
of woods, throw shadows closer.
Fields shorn short stir me to the present,
future layers of history.

At family dinners no one whispers
your name or that your mind's wound
still fattens the ebb and flow
of blood in our veins.

Climbing the ladder of night
to the half-moon, I find memory
of you in the dark side, a coarse cloth
I drag behind me through ashes.

Thanksgiving

. . . writing is like breathing and like prayer
— Elizabeth Christy

No time to wait for accolades,
you glide into the moment
that drives you to write,
the way wind rides the day
and pens its story.

Think of black-eyed susans
staring boldly into the sun,
goldfinch feeding frenzied
on thistle, rain
soothing drying leaves.

You tongue words, sweet
or sour puckering the mouth,
bite into a poem with the zest
of a salami and pickle sandwich,
cruise to the finish-high of tiramisu
or seven-sins chocolate cake.

Think of little rivers
burbling through gaps and rills
where language roils,
tugging on words, whirling syllables
like fall leaves.

You move words on the page, listen
for the tiny bell that rings
if a word snaps into the gap
of the puzzle that shapes your life —
a claret-red camelia bloom in November,
poetry its centered golden eye.

Day in Fall

. . . sound of inner stone
with heart on fire
— W. S. Merwin "The Rock"

Cloud shelves store your book of life.
Mine is still being written,
lacking the final chapter.

Shades only the sky can paint
remind me of your favorite oil on canvas —
a large sun divided in two,
metaphor for two sisters of one mind.

Now it hangs in your daughter's house
at the foot of a mountain castle.
We used to climb the rocky path,
stop on the way down
at the inn for bread and wine.

This morning a cardinal controls the feeder.
Squirrels bicker and chase each other
around the foot of a maple's golden crown.

I blow heart-shaped leaves
off the driveway, watch how they tumble
and disappear into the woods.

The past is like a stone.
Today it sings.

Weaving the Future

Maybe you are searching among the branches
for what only appears in the roots.
— Rumi

Lenten roses bloom purple fingertips
reminding when I squeeze mine for blood
after the needle prick
so the meter can measure my sweetness.

Hope lies in the roots we pass on,
our choices like branches
picked to weave toward the light.

Root blood loops through our bodies,
rushes toward open wounds,
the day's deeds: laws unraveled,
good restraints loosened, hope turned back.

Nightly, my ear hears the waning heartbeat
of a country as sleep's fingers ignite
tongues of light, moon crying blood
before the rooster's incessant crow.

Love is a Power Word

Last night a full moon stroked pines,
cooled the burning eye
of global warming.

The first leaves of fall tussle and tint
the pool's surface autumn-red,
stems sun-tinged.

A hummingbird nuzzles purple petunias,
skirting the lamp post
as if this drink were the last chance
to taste a cadence of summer.

Man-made poisons spread to berms
of butterfly staples, bird eggs,
air we breathe

while the enemy rising from the East
sharpens weapons
for our final battle.

Faith

Faith is the bird that feels the dawn
when the night is still dark.
— Rabindranath Tagore

Rain beats the windows,
burns back the clock
one hundred and thirty years.
As the Tennessee river rose,
covered low-lying fields and farms,
farmers fled chickens and pigs,
sorghum, maize, and cotton.

I listen to the pounding rain,
think of life's floods,
my belief that rain heals
the day's woes,
washes the world's dust off our souls.

Voles and possums know to burrow
deeper into earth.
Purple finches spread their feathers
over fledglings' cries for warmth.

Still, we stride strong winds
of hate, ignore rumbling thunder
hunching our shoulders
while lightning blitzes our tongues.

Morning's rainbow haloes the world,
covenants the promise
no other flood will drown us.
We are kindling for the fire.

Wildfire on Walden's Ridge

Kindled by drought
yesterday's brush sent bilious clouds
toward the city, bulged
neighborhood eaves, riddled lawns.

The harsh scent of burning roots
hung in the air, pressed
through muntins and door jambs,
lined our throats.

I saw Orion's belt buckled,
Ursa Major pulling her cart,
leaves drifting to the ground
as smoke traversed the night.

Voices brittle, throats dry,
our coughs bellow through the house,
heave our chests.

Last night raccoons channeled pine straw
for sunflower seeds, only found
maggots feasting.

Breathing

Crows patrol the sky's margin.
Peonies bloom blood-red.

Death's cape smothers troops at dusk
while the desert flickers
the sun's last whispers.

Watering window box impatiens,
I keep eyes on the nest
wedged between pots,
its three blue eggs. Cobweb-thin shells
easily cracked, ravaged.

Live shells explode on impact:
Twists of flame spiral,
curl bone and flesh, feather,
leave homes tangled
with sand and shrub.

After morning blossoms,
clouds brush the sky.
Wind wings dust over earth,
choking time.

Shadows, Darkening
for Joe

You belong to me,
even in the worst day.
Your text, *I have just a few weeks
to live.*

Stars recede, stop flickering
their secret codes
as this morning earth exhales,
and the soul grieves
that cancer frays your body.

I remember chasing you as toddler,
your grin and laughter
rounding a corner. Or at the creek
with pail and shovel
unearthing sand and pebbles.

You write, *burial is arranged
and the kids will live with relatives.*
You are too young for cancer
whittling down your will to live.

Perhaps like the deer
I watched at the knoll last night,
you will fade into the darkening woods
as the moon lights behind trees
and stars seed the sky.

September 9, 2001

Wind twirls birch leaves.
Soon they will whirl away
like butterflies. A willow hangs
its fingertips into the pond
where ducks open their beaks
to tossed bits of bread.
A blue heron and a turtle share
a log moored in brush.
A morning as peaceful
as cattails bending to breeze.

Stars Shine on Everyone

Gold bells of Carolina Jessamine
scent antebellum stairs of the tennis club.

A dinner for volunteers,
we crunch green salad,
nuzzle wine on the terrace.

Spring in February quivers,
throws a range of voices around us
like a warm cloak.

The evening star reigns the sky.
The river's mirror flickers, sways
city lights in rhythm

like our conversation of the new law
and how I carried luck in my luggage,
an immigrant fifty years ago.

A wall of clouds spreads the horizon.
I hear the pop pop pop
of balls in the courts below.

Laughter echoes through the trees,
still bare in their skeletons.

Beyond the stars, darkness hums.

Last Song

Getting from here to there
seems a simple exhale
of a frayed body, fluttering heart
spasming, winging air,
clinging to branches, rasping:
This is my story, this is my song.
Then the suck of celestial wind
reeling you in like silvery fish
in an ocean of clouds, stratosphere,
flung past the margins of death,
dropped into the wide arms of universe.
Caught in an ecstasy of flames,
a whirling flamenco, you are created,
wakened at your first cry.

Acknowledgements

The author would like to thank the editors of the following publications where some of the poems first appeared.

American Diversity Report: "Dance of the Forgotten," "Stars Shine on Everyone"
Aurorean: "Snow Moon"
Chattanooga Writers Guild: "Thanksgiving"
On the Veranda: "Blue"
Poetry South: "At St. Mary's Convent"
Poetry Quarterly: "Rivers of Living Water"
Slipstream: "Driving through Chickamauga Battlefield"
Streetlight Magazine: "Flash Flood"
Tipton Poetry Journal: "Loving the Dead"

Anthologies:
Carrying the Branch: Poets in Search of Peace: "*Je Suis Parisienne*"
Heart Rhythms: "Hungry Mother State Park"
Mizmor L'David: "Praise"

My sincerest thank you to Diane Frank for publishing this collection.

Another heartfelt thanks to KB Ballentine for her encouragement with this collection.

Thank you also to my Thursday night writing group.

Thank you to Melanie Gendron for her insightful design of this book.

About the Author

Helga Kidder is a native of Germany's Black Forest region and lives in the Tennessee hills with her husband. She was awarded an MFA in Writing from Vermont College. She is co-founder of the Chattanooga Writers Guild and leads their poetry group. She has participated in workshops in San Francisco, CA, Rockvale, TN, and Auvillar, France. Her poems have been published in many journals and anthologies. She has three poetry collections, *Wild Plums (*2012 Finishing Line Press*), Luckier than the Stars (*2013 Blue Light Press), and *Blackberry Winter* (2016 Blue Light Press).

Other books by Helga Kidder

Wild Plums (2012) Finishing Line Press

Luckier than the Stars (2013) Blue Light Press

Blackberry Winter (2016) Blue Light Press

www.ingramcontent.com/pod-product-compliance
Lightning Source LLC
Chambersburg PA
CBHW032027090426
42741CB00006B/763